I would like to dedicate this book to
my amazing wife and four incredible children
for allowing me to be silly and creative.
It's because of you that this
book is what it is today.

I love you all immensely.

Wall Dog
Publishing

The Adventures of Wall Dog and Shadow Cat
Written By: Jesse L. Stevenson
©2020 Wall Dog Publishing, LLC.

Night falls, and the stars in the sky
twinkle from above.
Dad hears a shout,
and when he gets to the bed,
it's Judi and Peety
wanting a story to be read.

"Dad! Can you read us a
bedtime story?" they so eagerly shout.
"No!" says dad.
As he walks over to turn off the light,
all of a sudden,
on the wall is a flash so bright.

As the kids become so afraid,
they lie on their backs.
Dad shouts, "Daht daht dahhhh!
It's the adventures of Wall Dog and Shadow Cat!"

Judi and Peety sit up with joy,
waiting for dad to tell tales to explore.

Once upon a time in a land called Wall,
was a kingdom so great
and a kingdom so tall!
There lived a people who needed a defender
for the good King Light Frog.

King Light Frog made a decree,
"We need a night watchman!" he shouted.
"One who is brave and courageous,
whose hugs and love are all contagious."

"The children are all scared
of the Shadow Cat.
We must protect them,
and that's a fact!"

Before King Light Frog could finish speaking,
there was a WISH! and a WASHEEE!
with the cutest of squeaking.
His ears were tall,
with his mouth he was panting.
Standing before the great King Light Frog
was the protector of the kingdom,
and his name was WALL DOG!

"YAY!" the people shouted.
Then all of a sudden,
the skies turned black.
The crowds of people feared the worst
when a sound so annoying came at first.
The people asked, "Is it a rat?"

Eyes red and tickle claws sharp,
his nose was stuffy and very flat.
He let out a yell,
"I am Shadow Cat!"
Afraid, the people ran to their homes
to call their hero, Wall Dog!

With a WISH! and a WASHEEE!
Wall Dog zipped in a flash.
"No, no, no, Shadow Cat!
You will not steal my tickles!
For I give them hugs and kisses
and warm nose sniffles!"

"Now be gone from the Kingdom of Light,
for you have been banned!
And return to your kingdom
of the Shadow Lands!"

Shadow Cat meowed as he turned and ran
and shouted, "Wall Dog! I am not your fan!
Keep your sniffles for another day,
for I'll be back, you hear?
Somehow. Some way!"

The citizens and the king were very happy.
King Light Frog said, "We're done! Thank you,
Wall dog. Now here is your bone.
We have won AGAIN!"

Now Judi and Peety are happy and sleepy. Dad tucks them in and gives a last sugar on the head and says, "Sleep well, babies, and have a wonderful rest."

The End

www.ingramcontent.com/pod-product-compliance
Lightning Source LLC
Chambersburg PA
CBHW040712150426

42811CB00061B/1855